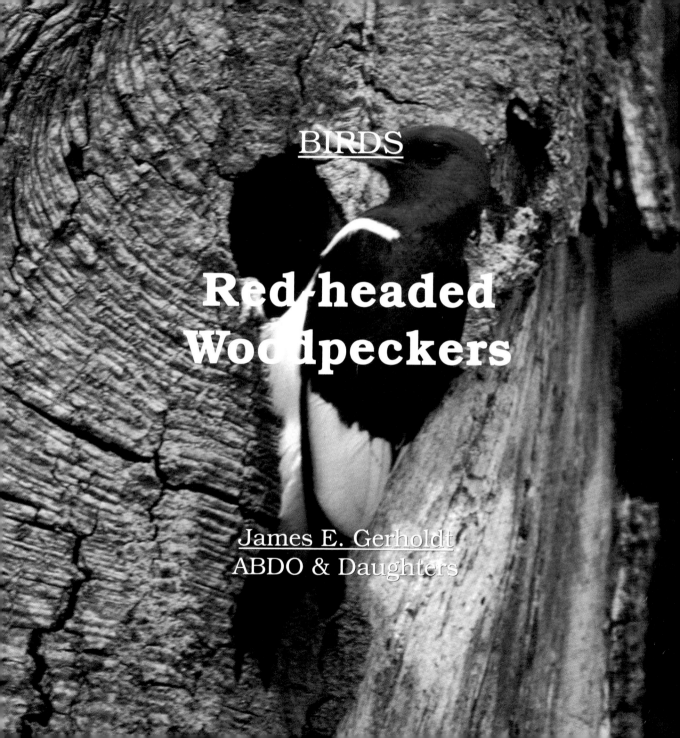

BIRDS

Red-headed Woodpeckers

James E. Gerholdt
ABDO & Daughters

Published by Abdo & Daughters, 4940 Viking Drive, Suite 622, Edina, Minnesota 55435.

Copyright © 1997 by Abdo Consulting Group, Inc., Pentagon Tower, P.O. Box 36036, Minneapolis, Minnesota 55435 USA. International copyrights reserved in all countries. No part of this book may be reproduced in any form without written permission from the publisher.

Printed in the United States.

Cover and Interior Photo credits: Peter Arnold, Inc.

Edited by Julie Berg

Library of Congress Cataloging-in-Publication Data

Gerholdt, James E., 1943—
      Red-headed woodpeckers/James E. Gerholdt.
         p.   cm. -- (birds)
      Includes index.
      Summary: Describes the physical characteristics, habits, and habitat of the birds known by the drumming sounds they make when boring into wood in search of food.
      ISBN 1-56239-588-2
      1. Red-headed woodpecker--Juvenile literature. [1. Red-headed woodpecker.
      2. Woodpeckers.] I. Title. II. Series: Gerholdt, James E., 1943—Birds.
      QL696.P56G47   1997
      598.7'2--dc20
                                           96-312
                                           CIP
                                           AC

Contents

RED-HEADED WOODPECKERS

Red-headed woodpeckers belong to one of the 28 **orders** of **birds**. They are called woodpeckers because they peck holes with their beaks into the trunks of trees and other wooden things—like fence posts—in search of food.

Birds are **vertebrates**. This means they have backbones, just like humans. Birds are also **warm-blooded**.

Red-headed woodpeckers are not as common as they once were. Many are killed by cars. Starlings use the same holes in trees for their nests that woodpeckers do—so many are left homeless.

The red-headed woodpecker.

SIZES

Red-headed woodpeckers are medium-sized **birds**. Their average weight is 2 1/2 to 3 ounces (70.5 to 85g).

From the tip of the beak to the tip of the tail, red-headed woodpeckers measure 8 1/2 to 9 1/2 inches (21.5 to 24cm). The **wingspan** is 16 to 18 inches (40.6 to 45.7cm).

Opposite page: A woodpecker in flight showing its wing size.

SHAPES

Red-headed woodpeckers are round-bodied **birds** with long, pointed tails. Like all woodpeckers, their tails are stiff, and are used to prop themselves against tree trunks.

The birds' beaks are long and straight, and very hard. They are used as a **chisel** to peck holes. The nostrils are covered with bristle-like **feathers** to keep dust out of their noses while pecking holes.

Red-headed woodpeckers have short legs. Their toes have sharp, curved nails to help them cling to the bark of tree trunks. Their feet have two toes pointing to the front, and two toes pointing to the back.

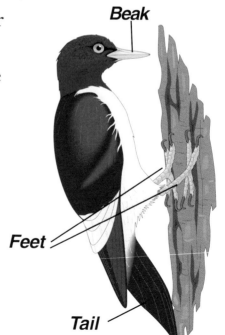

Beak

Feet

Tail

8

Woodpeckers have long,
pointy tails.

COLORS

Male and female red-headed woodpeckers have the same colors. The entire head is a bright red, which is how the woodpecker got its name. The neck and the upper **breast** are also bright red.

The back is solid black and the rump is white. There are large, square, white patches on the wings. The tail is black. Young red-headed woodpeckers have brownish-colored heads.

Opposite page: The red-headed woodpecker has a red head.

WHERE THEY LIVE

Red-headed woodpeckers are found east of the Rocky Mountains from southern Canada to the states along the Gulf of Mexico. But they are sometimes seen as far west as California, Arizona, Utah, and Idaho. In Canada, they may be seen as far west as British Columbia and Alberta.

Red-headed woodpeckers are found in open woods and prairie country. Some of their favorite places are **orchards** and shade trees. Look for them on the trunks of the trees.

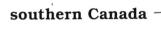
southern Canada

western United States

Gulf of Mexic

12

A gila woodpecker in Saguaro Park, Arizona.

SENSES

Red-headed woodpeckers have the same five senses as humans. Their senses of taste and smell are not very good. But these senses are not very important to them.

Red-headed woodpeckers have good eyesight, which helps them find food in the air or on the ground. Their sense of hearing also helps them find food. A buzzing insect may be heard before it is seen!

The sense of hearing also helps the red-headed woodpecker to find a **mate**, either with its song or the drumming sound on a tree trunk or post.

Opposite page: The woodpecker's eyesight is good.

DEFENSE

Because they pick insects from roads, red-headed woodpeckers have an **enemy** that most **birds** do not—the automobile! Many are hit by cars as they swoop down to grab food.

Bird-eating **predators** are also dangerous. However, the woodpeckers' unusual flight—several wingbeats followed by a swoop with the wings closed—makes it difficult for enemies to catch them.

Opposite page: A woodpecker in flight.

FOOD

Insects are among the red-headed woodpecker's favorite food. Most are caught in the air, on the ground, or in shrubs. Some of these food insects are ants, wasps, beetles, weevils, spiders, and centipedes.

Unlike most woodpeckers, the red-headed woodpecker rarely drills into trees to find food. But they do drill into dead wood for grubs.

Red-headed woodpeckers also like vegetables. These include corn, berries, cherries, and acorns.

Opposite page: A woodpecker searching a flower for an insect meal.

BABIES

All red-headed woodpeckers **hatch** from eggs with smooth, white shells. The eggs are small, and only measure 1 by 3/4 inches (25 by 19mm).

Five eggs are often laid at one time. But sometimes as many as eight are laid.

The nest is built in a hole that has been **chiseled** out by the parents. This hole is made in dead trees, or stumps, and sometimes in telephone poles or fence posts.

The nest may be as high as 80 feet (24m) or as low as the ground. The babies hatch after about two weeks. They leave the nest when they are about one month old.

Opposite page: An adult woodpecker feeding the baby woodpeckers.

GLOSSARY

bird (BURD) - A feathered animal with a backbone whose front limbs are wings.

breast - The front part of a bird's body; the chest.

chisel (CHIZ-ull) - To cut or shape a hole in wood.

enemy - Something dangerous or harmful to something else.

feather (FETH-ur) - The light, flat structures covering a birds body.

hatch - To come forth or be born from an egg.

mate - The male or female of a pair of animals.

orchard - An area where fruit or nut trees are grown.

order (OAR-der) - A grouping of animals.

predator (PREAD-a-tore) - An animal that eats other animals.

vertebrate (VER-tuh-brit) - An animal with a backbone.

warm-blooded (warm BLUD-ed) - Regulating body temperature at a constant level, from inside the body.

wingspan (WING-span) - The distance from the tip of one wing to the other.

INDEX